WALKING TOGETHER
Steps to Discipleship

Dennis Craig

Energion Publications
Cantonment, FL
2024

Cover Design: Henry E. Neufeld

ISBN: 978-1-63199-907-9
eISBN: 978-1-63199-908-6

Energion Publications
1241 Conference Rd
Cantonment, FL 32533

pubs@energion.com
energion.com

Table of Contents

The purpose of this Study

A pastor was telling a story one time about a little girl whose greatest wish was to see the ocean. It was all she talked about – the waves, the sunshine, the sand between her toes. She begged her mom and dad year after year for the family to take a trip to the ocean. Finally, for her eighth birthday, her mom and dad gave her the amazing news that she was finally going to see the ocean.

She could barely contain her excitement as she crossed off the days on the calendar. Finally, the day arrived, and it was all she could do to remain seated in the car and not try and get out and push so they would get there faster.

Then suddenly, they were there. She was standing in front of the majesty of God's creation, seeing all she had dreamed of. She ran, laughed, and squealed while she was jumping and splashing in the water. She ventured out until the water was about mid-thigh. Her parents were not worried since she was an excellent swimmer.

Out of nowhere a big ol' wave came along and just absolutely wiped her out. She came up out of the water crying, sputtering, and spitting water out of her mouth. She had not fallen hard but nonetheless she just would not stop crying. Her dad asked her why she was so upset. She looked up and said accusingly, "You always told me how wonderful it would be at the ocean, but you never told me what to do once I got here!"

The church of today has made a pretty big error. We have told a generation how amazing it is to find Jesus and how awesome salvation is. But we forget to answer the ultimate question – Now what???

If you feel that way, then I hope this study is just what you are looking for. You have just made an amazing, life-changing decision by giving your life to God and accepting Jesus as your Savior. I do not even know you personally, but I am so amazingly excited for you and cannot wait to see what God has in store for you as you walk with Him. You are probably feeling some amazing feelings right now, but you are also probably overwhelmed with uncertainty about what exactly just happened and more importantly, what comes next?

That is what Walking Together-Steps to Discipleship is all about. This is intended to be a different kind of 12-steps program. Walking Together is designed to help guide you from your salvation experience to an understanding of what it really means to walk in your true purpose and calling as a disciple of God.

Will it be easy? No. Are you going to face some tough questions and conversations? Yes. However, I will be here with you every step of the way as you explore God's word and His calling in your life. At the end of this book is my personal e-mail address. I would love to hear your thoughts, feelings, and questions as you study along. Get ready to be blessed as you begin to connect not only with the Spirit dwelling within you, but hopefully to connect with other believers in your community who are walking the same road right alongside of you.

Hang on.... It is going to be an amazing ride.

-- Dennis Craig

Therefore, if anyone is in Christ, the new creation has come: The old has gone, the new is here!
2 Corinthians 5:17

Well, every journey has a starting point. When it comes to our steps towards purpose, it all starts with salvation. Salvation is a very fancy word which to all of us average everyday people simply means to be saved from our sin. You see, in the beginning God created us to have a relationship with Him. When Adam sinned, this separated us from God and made it necessary for man to die as payment for sin.

Jesus, God's only son, came as a sacrifice to pay that penalty so that we did not have to be separated from God any longer.

Did you hear that? It is already paid. It is already forgiven. You do not have to be separated anymore. But you do have to do a few things.

1. **You must admit that you are a sinner and that you need God's help.** Romans 3:23: *For all have sinned and fallen short of the glory of God.*

   Yes, you heard me. You are a sinner. I am a sinner. We are all sinners. There is not a person alive that can claim to have lived a righteous life except for one, Jesus. We cannot with our own strength overcome our sin...we need Jesus.

2. **You must believe that Jesus is God's Son and that He came and died for YOU.** 1 Timothy 1:15 (NLT): *This is a trustworthy saying, and everyone should accept it: "Christ Jesus came into the world to save sinners"—and I am the worst of them all."*

Jesus came because the Father could not live without YOU anymore. If you were the only person who ever sinned, Jesus would have bled and died for you. A great friend of mine said, "God does not give bad for good. He would not exchange something of greater value for something of lesser value, and he gave up his SON for YOU.

3. **You must repent of your sin and accept Jesus as your Lord and Savior.** 1 John 1:9: *If we confess our sins, he is faithful and just and will forgive us our sins and purify us from all unrighteousness.*

    You must own what you are to become what you are supposed to be. You cannot heal something if you conceal it. To repent of something means you must TURN in the opposite direction from where you are going. Turn from dark to light, from sin to righteousness, and go from hopelessness to the hope found in Christ. The first step to do that is to admit your sin to the ONE who can take it all away.

4. **You have to confess with your mouth that Jesus is Lord. This means you must tell others about Him and what He has done for you.** Romans 10:9: *If you declare with your mouth, "Jesus is Lord," and believe in your heart that God raised him from the dead, you will be saved.*

    Salvation stops being private the MOMENT that you accept Christ into your heart. The final command of Christ was to "Go into all the world and preach the gospel to every creature." TELL OTHERS what God has done in you. Spread the good news that you have received!!!!!

For many of you, the reason that you are starting this program is that you have already done what is described above. You admitted your need for God, and you accepted Him. But for the next eleven steps to matter, you need to really understand what that means for you.

YOU are starting over. God has sent His spirit to dwell within you. You are getting the ultimate do-over. Those things which have held you back have no more power.

YOU ARE BRAND NEW. You are a new creation. Chip and Joanna Gaines have nothing on the makeover you have just experienced. God has cleaned you from the inside out and set you on a new road.

YOU ARE BRAND NEW. Like the prodigal son, you were lost but now you are found. You were blind, but now you see.

YOU ARE BRAND NEW. The old you is gone. You may still think that the old person is still there, but the Bible tells us that God has removed your sin as far as the east is from the west and He remembers it no more.

YOU ARE BRAND NEW.

DEEP DIVE QUESTIONS

- How have I changed since receiving my salvation? Write down the differences you can see and feel! Use this list as a reminder of how you are DIFFERENT now that Christ lives in you!
- What does it REALLY mean to be made new? Think this through. I know it sounds like a simple question, but once something is made, it is considered complete. How can it be made new again? **John 3:1-21**
- Have you truly repented of the person you USED to be? You have heard it said that sometimes it takes more than "I'm sorry" to really be effective. Repenting is not just the words, but an ACTION of turning away. Have you?

NOTES

> *And do not be conformed to this world, but be transformed by the renewing of your mind, that you may prove what is that good and acceptable and perfect will of God.*
> Romans 12:2 (NKJV)

Beginning this journey to walking in your purpose starts in a difficult place. We learned in week one that accepting the salvation of God in Christ Jesus is truly gaining an understanding that we are a new creation. Becoming this new creation starts in the mind.

Renewing the mind is a process.

1. **First, we must realize that God graced us with free will, and with that will, we can choose those things in our world that are glorifying to God.** Philippians 4:8 tells us that *"whatever is true, whatever is just, whatever is pure, whatever is lovely, whatever is commendable, if there is any excellence, if there is anything worthy of praise, think about these things."* We must choose, every day, to think of good and Godly things.

    You may not think you are able to, but you can absolutely gain control over your mind. 2 Corinthians 10:5 tells us that *"We demolish arguments and every pretension that sets itself up against the knowledge of God, and we take captive every thought to make it obedient to Christ."* When you accept Christ into your life, the Holy Spirit takes up residence within you. This means that you have a power within you that is stronger than any negativity, anxiety, depression, or anger which threatens to come into your mind.

Colossians 3:1-4 (NLT) tells us where to place our thoughts and our sights, *"Since you have been raised to new life with Christ, set your sights on the realities of heaven, where Christ sits in the place of honor at God's right hand. Think about the things of heaven, not the things of earth. For you died to this life, and your real life is hidden with Christ in God. And when Christ, who is your life, is revealed to the whole world, you will share in all his glory."* Did you catch that last, best part? YOU WILL SHARE IN HIS GLORY!!!!!

2. **Next, we must take steps to guard against what we are putting into our minds.** We live in a world where acceptance and self-worth are measured in likes, views, and followers on social media. We accept the evil that surrounds us as entertainment as it assaults our eyes, ears, and memories. We claim to be new creations, but we constantly dive into conversations and activities which have always been a part of who we WERE, and which consistently pull us away from our intended purpose and from our newfound freedom in Christ.

Colossians 3:5-11 (NLT) continues with this message *"So put to death the sinful, earthly things lurking within you. Have nothing to do with sexual immorality, impurity, lust, and evil desires. Don't be greedy, for a greedy person is an idolater, worshiping the things of this world. Because of these sins, the anger of God is coming. You used to do these things when your life was still part of this world. But now is the time to get rid of anger, rage, malicious behavior, slander, and dirty language. Don't lie to each other, for you have stripped off your old sinful nature and all its wicked deeds. Put on your new nature and be renewed as you learn to know your Creator and become like him. In this new life, it doesn't matter if you are a Jew or a Gentile, circumcised or uncircumcised, barbaric, uncivilized, slave, or free. Christ is all that matters, and he lives in all of us."*

To give it some context: Continuing to think and act the way you did before is like staying in your sweaty gym clothes after a workout. The stench stays on you. Put on fresh garments which have been cleaned, pressed, and prepared by Christ for us. Get rid of the filth that threatens to invade your mind. Guard your mind just as much, if not more, than you would your body.

3. **Once you empty your mind of the old and guard against it returning, you must fill it with something new!!!** We must soak our minds with the Word of God. Colossians 3:16 (NKJV) says, *"Let the word of Christ dwell in you richly."* We will only see God and His Son more if we search the Word because that is where They can be found.

My daughter is a huge fan of hot tea. I would rather drink straight vinegar than hot tea, but that is beside the point. Anyone who is a tea-drinker will tell you that the longer you let the tea bag steep in the hot water, the stronger the tea will be. The same goes with diving into the Word of God. The longer you let yourself soak in the scriptures, the stronger the Word will reign in your mind and life.

4. **Finally, finish the transformation by speaking truth to your spirit to replace the lies that you have lived in most of your life.** The words you say have incredible power. According to Proverbs 18:21, *"The tongue has the power of life and death."*

Realize who you TRULY ARE by recognizing the love your Father has for you. Ephesians 3:17b-19 says, *"I pray that you, being rooted and established in love, may have power, together with all the Lord's holy people, to grasp how wide and long and high and deep is the love of Christ, and to know this love that surpasses knowledge—that you may be filled to the measure of all the fullness of God."*

Your words can either speak life or death to your own spirit, and for true transformation to take place, these words of life must be so ingrained in us that we live them out through our actions.

DEEP DIVE QUESTIONS

- What thoughts in your mind need replacing? If your answer is zero, then I highly suggest having a gut-check moment. Remember, remove all negativity, all malice, all lust, all lies.
- What is the best and worst thing about free will? I know it feels like a trick question, but it is not. Having free will sometimes is difficult. Sometimes, wouldn't it just be easier for God to say, "DO THIS!" But he doesn't, it has to be our choice.
- What words of life do you need to start speaking over yourself? How does your self-image impact your ability to see yourself as forgiven and free? How can speaking those words CHANGE your self-image?

NOTES

_____

_____

_____

_____

_____

_____

> *So this is my command: Love each other deeply, as much as I have loved you. For the greatest love of all is a love that sacrifices all. And this great love is demonstrated when a person sacrifices his life for his friends.*
>
> *You show that you are my intimate friends when you obey all that I command you. I have never called you 'servants,' because a master doesn't confide in his servants, and servants don't always understand what the master is doing. But I call you my most intimate and cherished friends, for I reveal to you everything that I've heard from my Father.*
> John 15:12-15 (TPT)

One of the hardest parts about stepping into purpose is realizing that Jesus did not just forgive you of your sins, but He also calls you His friend. He not only loves you, but He desires intimacy with you.

You might be thinking, "Well, that doesn't seem too hard." The problem is that many of us are aware of our pasts, our failures, and our weaknesses. We think that if we do not love ourselves, how can God want us in His family?

The strange thing is we have no problem believing the people of this world love us. We have no problem believing our "feelings." Whether it was the puppy love of our youth, whatever it was we called it in our late-teen and college years, or sadly the toxic relationships many of us have experienced as adults. We always managed to convince ourselves it was love every time, only to have it proven that it was not.

Our past experiences have made it difficult to imagine that the Creator of the Universe would want to be close to us, or that He trusts us with a purpose, or that He would love us.

He does. He does. He does.

In fact, He loves us SO MUCH that He committed the ultimate act of love by laying down His life for us, His friends. He stepped down from the throne room, put on flesh, and died in the most horrible way imaginable just so He would not have to spend eternity without us.

In the most often-quoted verse ever written, John 3:16 (NKJV) it tells us that *"For God so loved the world that He gave His only begotten Son, that whoever believes in Him should not perish but have everlasting life."* Just like we pass around food at Thanksgiving or share a hug with a brother or sister, we should also share this same love with all around us.

We must realize we are a part of a family. A "great cloud of witnesses" as the scriptures say. We are a part of a family whose number knows no end. We must do all we can to increase that family. The greatest step is to trust the excellent work that He has done in us and to share it with those whom we love and who need it the most.

I do not know about you, but sometimes my family drives me crazy. We argue and fight like cats and dogs over everything from politics to religion to the best way to cook a turkey. However, I can tell you directly that I would do anything to protect my family from even one moment of pain or difficulty.

The family you now belong to is meant to be very much the same. We are meant to stand together when storms rage and when Satan starts to throw those fiery darts at us. We are meant to be an army, marching together to advance the Kingdom of God on this earth. How do we do that? We love one another as Christ first loved us.

So, if no one else has said it to you, let me: Welcome to the Family.

DEEP DIVE QUESTIONS

- Why is it hard for some believers to truly trust that God loves them?
- Why is it easier sometimes to trust and believe in strangers more than our own families?
- As a believer, what could you be doing more to increase this family, and our "Great Cloud of Witnesses?"

NOTES

_____

_____

_____

_____

_____

_____

_____

_____

_____

> *"Then he said to me, 'The God of our ancestors*
> *has destined you to know his plan and for you to see*
> *the Holy One and to hear his voice. For you will be*
> *his witness to every race of people and will share with*
> *them everything that you have seen and heard. So*
> *now, what are you waiting for? Get up, be baptized,*
> *and wash away your sins as you call upon his name.'"*
> Acts 22:14-16 (TPT)

So, up to this point, you have taken the steps to accept God's gift of salvation, to strive to renew your mind, and accept the reality that you are now a part of a family. The time has come to change your steps from inward reflection to outward declaration.

The act of repentance and salvation is by its nature a very cleansing act. The Bible tells us in Isaiah 1:18 (TPT) that, *"Though your sins stain you like scarlet, I will whiten them like bright, new-fallen snow!"* When we accept God's salvation, our sin is removed, and we move from death to life.

Baptism is the perfect expression of this cleansing and resurrection. Romans 6:3-4 declares, *"Or don't you know that all of us who were baptized into Christ Jesus were baptized into His death? We were therefore buried with him through baptism into death in order that, just as Christ was raised from the dead through the glory of the Father, we too may live a new life."*

Baptism is an outward and visible sign of an invisible grace. It is our way of declaring to the world that a change has taken place in the heart of a believer. Galatians 3:27 (NLT) says, *"And all who have been united with Christ in baptism have put on Christ, like putting on new clothes."* The Word instructs us to make this declaration to the world by leaving it all in the water. To allow our past, our sins, our mistakes, our fears, and our worries to wash away and to rise as a NEW CREATION.

How important is your baptism? It is your personal identification with the greatest act of human history—the death, burial, and resurrection of Jesus Christ. Baptism does not save you—salvation comes by faith alone. The thief on the cross is evidence of that, as he was not baptized yet was with Christ that day in paradise. Your guilt before God is removed the moment you trust in Christ. But baptism is your personal testimony to, and the inward assurance of, your passage from the old life to the new life.

TAKE THE LEAP. Make the decision to take this amazing experience that you have been having and declare it to the world. Take the steps up to the water and dive in, never to be the same again.

DEEP DIVE QUESTIONS

- Have you considered being baptized? Why or why not?
- What is it in your spirit that needs to be "left in the water?"
- To you, what does baptism symbolize?

NOTES

_____

_____

_____

_____

_____

_____

_____

_____

_____

_____

_____

_____

Well, we have spent four lessons discussing what salvation really means, how to renew our mind, that we are part of an amazing new family, and finally how to make the public declaration of the change which has taken place within.

Recently I was cast in our local theatre production of Meredith Wilson's Broadway musical, "The Music Man." In this musical, con-man Harold Hill proclaims that he could form a boys' band that could play successfully without ever needing to rehearse or even touch their instruments. He claimed that he could use what he calls, "The Think System," and they would be able to play the music simply by THINKING about it. As in most cases with musicals, the kids ended up being able to magically play their instruments and there was a happy ending.

Christianity and Discipleship is not a "think system." Salvation comes by faith, but to call yourself a Christian means to be "Christ-like" – This requires ACTION!

Now, we are going to spend the next four weeks talking about what an active Christian lifestyle involves. Christianity is not a sedentary undertaking. Christ's last words as he rose to heaven were for His followers to GO into all the world and preach and baptize and lead others to HIM.

We will dive into the four areas of Christian life that we as believers are not just invited, but encouraged to participate in:

- Prayer – prayer is our most powerful tool as a Christian because it allows us to communicate DIRECTLY with the Father.
- Presence – For us to walk into purpose, we must SHOW UP.

- Gifts – We have to give of ourselves. Tithing and giving of our financial gain is a mandate from the Father for all who love Him.
- Service – No one who calls himself or herself a Christian can just stand on the sideline. We must get in the game and be a part of serving others.

Those of you who grew up in the United Methodist Church may recognize those four steps, as they were a popular motto for the church in the 90s and early 2000's. While I may have left that denomination years ago, I cannot deny the truth of those four little words that direct us to a life of action for Christ.

So, let's dive in.

> *"Don't worry about anything; instead, pray about everything. Tell God what you need, and thank Him for all He has done. Then you will experience God's peace, which exceeds anything we can understand. His peace will guard your hearts and minds as you live in Christ Jesus."*
> Philippians 4:6-8 (NLT)

In the beginning, God walked in the garden with Adam and Eve. Once sin came into the picture, God desired connection with His children. Prayer is how God taught His kids to communicate with Him.

Prayer is direct contact with the divine. At its heart, it is God's way of allowing us to love, praise, plead with, and give our love to Him every day. The scripture tells us that God inhabits the praises of His people. (Psalm 22:3, KJV) This shows us that when we go to God through prayer and adoration, He inhabits that adoration. He dwells within our prayers and praises!

Developing a full prayer life should be one of the first desires of a new Christian. Prayer is the center of everything. Happy – pray to praise Him. Scared – pray for peace. In desperate need – cry out to Him in prayer.

There are many kinds of prayer, but we can break the majority into five categories.

1. **Adoration** - Prayers which Praise God simply for who He is – We pray to God to praise Him for His greatness and admit our dependence on Him. Mark 12:30 (NKJV) – *"And you shall love the Lord your God with all your heart, and with all your soul, and with all your mind, and with all your strength."*

2. **Confessions -** Prayers which confess our sins to God –
    We use prayer to own up to our sin and ask for God's
    mercy and forgiveness. 1 John 1:9 (NKJV) – *"If we con-
    fess our sins, He is faithful and just to forgive us our sins
    and to cleanse us from all unrighteousness.*

3. **Thanksgiving -** Prayers which thank God for what He
    has done – Thanking God for His many blessings, such
    as health or children. 1 Thessalonians 5:16-18 – *"Rejoice
    always, pray continuously, give thanks in all circum-
    stances; for this is God's will for you in Christ Jesus."*

4. **Petition -** Prayers which ask for things from God –
    Asking God for something, such as healing, courage, or
    discernment. Ephesians 6:18 (NASB) – *"With all prayer
    and petition pray at all times in the Spirit, and with this
    in view, be on the alert with all perseverance and peti-
    tion for all the saints."*

5. **Intercession -** Prayers on behalf of the needs of oth-
    ers – Asking God to help others who need it, such as
    the sick, poor, the suffering, and those who have not
    accepted God's forgiveness. James 5:14 – *"Is anyone
    among you sick? Then he must call for the elders of the
    church and they are to pray over him, anointing him
    with oil in the name of the Lord."*

All these types of prayers must focus on one of two
things: Edifying the body of Christ, or glorifying God. We
are forgiven, healed, and brought closer to God not for our
own glory, but for His.

Deepening your prayer life is not for the faint of
heart. It is direct contact with the almighty Creator of the
universe. Prayer changes us, fulfills us, and takes us into
deeper realms of the Spirit than we ever thought possible.

However, let me say this. There are two rules to prayer
that many Christians do not realize, and it causes extreme
frustration when things may not turn out the way they
hoped.

1.   **Be aware of your motivation.**

God hears every prayer – this means that we should be aware of why we are asking for what we are asking for. As was stated before, the purposes of prayer are to achieve intimacy with God, edify the body, and glorify God and His Son, Jesus. We need to be aware of our motives when we entreat the God of the heavens.

2.   **God can say no.**

That does not sound right does it. It is natural to think that if our motives are pure and if we desire to build up others, grow the Kingdom, and glorify God that He should say yes to our requests and give us what we ask for. That is not how it works.

Approaching God is recognizing that He is so much bigger than anything we can comprehend. His will does not always make sense to us. His purposes will always stand, and sometimes, even the purest of requests does not fit in the plan of an infinite God. He is allowed to say no.

When these moments happen, it is important for us to realize why we approached God in the first place. He loves us and desires nothing but our good. His ways are higher, greater, deeper, and better. We will not always understand them, and sometimes, it will hurt. Nevertheless, it is better.

Prayer allows us an amazing opportunity. We get to talk with, laugh with, cry with, and communicate with the very one who made us.

So, the next time you pray. Do not worry whether your words are fancy or that you are saying the "right thing." Go to the one that made you. Go with a broken heart and a contrite spirit and trust that if the One that created you loves you enough to die for you, then He will listen to your heart and your words and WILL always do what is best for you, His child.

DEEP DIVE QUESTIONS

- When you pray, which of the five types of prayer (Adoration, Confession, Thanksgiving, Petition, Intercession) do you find yourself doing the most?
- Do you find it easy to pray? Or, do you find yourself struggling with what to say or how to say it? After reading the lesson today, why do you think that is?
- What is your usual reaction when something you pray for does not work out?

NOTES

_____

_____

_____

_____

_____

_____

_____

"This is not the time to pull away and neglect meeting together, as some have formed the habit of doing. In fact, we should come together even more frequently, eager to encourage and urge each other onward as we anticipate that day dawning."
Hebrews 10:25 (TPT)

How many times have we heard someone (even ourselves) say, "You don't need to go to church to be a Christian?" People for centuries have lived out their lives with a heart set against organized religion. They have done everything they can to stay out of church, while still professing to believe in Jesus.

It may surprise you to know that they are correct. You can claim faith in Christ and receive salvation without ever stepping foot in a church. However, God does not just want us to live a basic faith. Christ did not die for us to have a basic faith. Most of all, Jesus did not tell his followers at his ascension to model and experience a basic faith.

Jesus desires us to have abundantly more than all we ask or imagine. He wants us to live out our Christian walk in extraordinary ways TOGETHER. In 1 Corinthians 12, Paul tells us that our bodies are composed of many parts and that ALL those parts are necessary for the body to function. The church, as the body of Christ, is the same.

To receive all that God has for us, we as His followers need to SHOW UP. We need to be present for God to use us daily. Sitting at home reading the Word, praying, and singing songs may grow our own faith, but Christ commands us to share the good news of the Gospel. He commands us to march together in this battle for our friends, family, and those whom we have not even met yet that need Him.

In Hebrews, God's word instructs us to be involved with a church, community, or fellowship of believers. But why? Why is this important?

1. **The church was God's idea.**
   It may not look exactly as Christ intended, but the church was God's plan to accomplish His work on earth today. God uses so many words to describe the church: his bride, the household of God, and the body of Christ. What they all have in common is that they tell us that the church is important to God.

2. **The church is where God's people learn about Him**
   The Bible tells us that the church is meant to teach God's word to His children. Yes, we have the internet, videos, podcasts, and other sources now. Listen close - nothing beats sitting amongst other believers listening to a God-called preacher reveal the deeper truths of the Word.

3. **The Church is God's arena for believers to develop their spiritual gifts.**
   The Church was never meant to be a concert or performance. It was meant to be a place where believers can find the spiritual gifts which they are blessed with and be TRAINED and ENCOURAGED to use them actively. Church is not passive spectating....it is active participation.

4. **The Church is where believers find community.**
   Nowhere in the scriptures does the Bible tell us to love ourselves, pray for ourselves, forgive ourselves, or lead ourselves to faith in Christ. However, it tells us dozens of times to do that for others. James 5:16 (NLT) tells us to *"confess your sins to one another and pray for each other so that you may be healed."* It is hard to do that all by yourself. Young believers need older, more experienced Christians to mentor and teach them and older Christians need to see the fire and excitement of the "baby Christians" sometimes to keep their own faith fresh.

5. **The Church is God's outlet for reaching the lost.**

Since the early church in the book of Acts, the purpose of the church was clear – Build the Kingdom. God used the Church to care for the widows, orphans, and the lost. They combined their wealth and took care of the less fortunate. They sent out missionaries and did all they could to complete the Great Commission to preach the gospel to every creature. When they worked together in community, the Bible tells us that they saw their numbers increase daily. That could not be accomplished without the fellowship of believers.

To be more like Christ, we must walk in community with others. Jesus was the Son of God. He was righteous, holy, and capable of performing miracles. He also chose a group of people to walk with Him through His ministry. He knew that He would be even more effective by communing with not only His father, but also the family He surrounded himself with daily. He broke bread with these people. He laughed and cried with these people. The one person that could have done it alone chose not to.

The idea is as old as the mountains. We are stronger together than apart. God's word tells us in Ecclesiastes 4:12 that *"Though one may be overpowered, two can defend themselves. A cord of three strands is not quickly broken."* Christ understood this; He surrounded himself with not just followers, but friends. Here is the best part - He chose the weird, downtrodden, broken screw-ups of the world. I do not know about you, but that lets me know that He could choose me too.

With God's Spirit dwelling within us, He made sure that we have everything we need to survive this world and be with Him forever. With the fellowship of believers that surround us, He made sure that we have everything we need to not just live but live abundantly.

Deep Dive Questions

- Why do you think so many people have a bad taste in their mouth about being a part of a church?
- Do you have a community - a group of people that you feel you can walk through anything with?
  - If yes, what qualities do the people that you choose to be in community with share?
  - If not, why do you think that is?
- How have others helped you to live a more abundant life?

NOTES

_____

_____

_____

_____

_____

_____

_____

*"Bring all the tithes into the storehouse so there
will be enough food in my temple. If you do," says the
Lord of Heaven's Armies, "I will open the windows of
heaven for you. I will pour out a blessing so great you
won't have enough room to take it in! Try it! Put me
to the test!"*
Malachi 3:10 (NLT)

No one in the history of Christian leadership likes to
talk about money. No pastor in the history of the
church ever liked to preach about tithing. No one
writing a study on the steps toward discipleship enjoys
writing about tithing. But let me tell you a secret:

Tithing is one of the most important things a Christian
can do.

In the above verse in Malachi, you get to witness something that happens only one time in all sixty-six books of
the Bible. God says to put Him to the test. He dares us to
let Him bless us. All that He requires is for us to give back
only a portion of what is His.

"What do you mean it is his? I worked hard for the
money I make!" I can hear the thoughts flowing through
your minds right now.

Let me ask you a few questions. Who blessed you with
talents, intelligence, and abilities? God did. Who then provided you with a job? God did. Who continuously watches
over you and makes sure that you and your family are ok?
God does. All that we have is simply a result of the gifts
and graces of God.

A tithe is ten percent of what we bring in. Proverbs
3:9-10 (NKJV) says, *"Honor the Lord with your possessions,
and with the first fruits of all your increase; so your barns
will be filled with plenty, and your vats will overflow with*

new wine." Our tithes are these first fruits that the proverb speaks of. As a Christian, one of the most important steps we can take is coming to the realization that tithing is not just something we do; it is an act of obedience and worship. It is a blessing to be able to give back to our Father.

2 Corinthians 9:6-9 says *"Remember this: Whoever sows sparingly will also reap sparingly, and whoever sows generously will also reap generously. Each of you should give what you have decided in your heart to give, not reluctantly or under compulsion, for God loves a cheerful giver. And God is able to bless you abundantly, so that in all things at all times, having all that you need, you will abound in every good work."*

As hard as it is, God asks us to be a cheerful giver. Yes, you heard me correctly. Every Christian finds it hard to have a cheerful heart when giving back ten percent of what we earn. We see the bills that could be paid with that money. We see fun things we could do or buy. We see food, gifts, and vacations. However, God sees what we do not see.

Do you know why God tells us to be cheerful givers? He knows our faith will grow as He continues to *"supply all of our needs according to His riches in Glory"* as it says in Philippians 4:19 (NASB). God sees the blessings that He promised in Malachi to pour out. God sees ministries with enough financial support to pour into the lives of the lost and broken. God sees our love for Him when we give generously in response to His grace and presence in our lives.

"But even if I tithe, I can only afford like $10."

In Mark 12:41-44 it says, *"Jesus sat down opposite the place where the offerings were put and watched the crowd putting their money into the temple treasury. Many rich people threw in large amounts. But a poor widow came and put in two small copper coins, worth only a few cents.*

Calling his disciples to him, Jesus said, "Truly I tell you, this poor widow has put more into the treasury than all the others. They all gave out of their wealth; but she, out of her poverty, put in everything—all she had to live on."

Do not let your current situation determine how you feel about tithing. Jesus told us in the parable that the widow that gave two little copper coins gave more than the rich man ever could, because she gave all she had. God does not want millions of dollars, folks. He just wants all you can give because He gave all for you.

Deep Dive Questions

- What has stopped you from tithing in the past?
- Have you ever really viewed tithing as an act of worship? Why or why not?
- What should determine how much you give to the body of Christ? Your faith, or your circumstances? Now, answer what has been determining it for you?

NOTES

_____

_____

_____

_____

_____

_____

_____

_____

Week 8 – Service

Every believer has received grace gifts, so use them to serve one another as faithful stewards of the many-colored tapestry of God's grace. For example, if you have a speaking gift, speak as though God were speaking His words through you. If you have the gift of serving, do it passionately with the strength God gives you, so that in everything, God alone will be glorified through Jesus Christ.
1 Peter 4: 10-11 (TPT)

Well, as the old faithful statement goes, "It's time to put up or shut up." Many of you reading this are active members of the congregations where you are doing this study. What I mean by that is you come every week, hear challenging and uplifting sermons, get swept up in the worship, and then you go home. It is time to start taking what you have learned and start giving back. In other words...put up or shut up.

Why is serving God so important? Why is serving others so important? Great questions! I am so glad you asked.

The first thing as Christians we need to realize is that we were created to do two things – glorify God and edify the body. In other words, a Christian's main purpose on earth is to increase God's kingdom on this earth AND in heaven. We do this by building up the body of Christ...... the Church.

As we learned in Week 2 of this booklet, God created each of us with unique gifts, talents, personalities, and skill sets. We get the most joy and make the biggest difference for God when we use our God-given talents, gifts, and abilities to build the church.

Serving God gives us blessings beyond measure. Yes, we are blessed to sit in the sanctuary and hear great teachings and music and by experiencing fellowship, but until we begin to serve others, our blessings will be limited.

Here are some real blessings we receive by serving others:

1. **Serving God lets us discover and develop our spiritual gifts.**

   As we read in 1 Corinthians 12, just as the human body is made up of different parts, we are all given different abilities and skills. Alone, these pieces are not particularly useful, but together, they can change the world.

2. **Serving allows us to experience miracles.**

   The greatest example of this is the wedding in Canaan. Jesus turned water into wine, but the guests had no idea what happened. It was the servants who witnessed the miracle first-hand.

3. **Serving allows us to be more like Jesus.**

   When we serve, we shift our focus from us to others. When we help others, we start to see others as Jesus sees them. When we get down in the muck and mire of this world to reach others, it gives us an entirely new perspective. Matthew 25:40 (ESV) — *"And the King will answer them, "Truly, I say to you, as you did it to one of the least of these my brothers, you did it to me."*

4. **Serving increases our faith.**

   Serving others requires that we move out of our comfort zone, which requires tremendous faith. By doing this, we see what God can do in us when we let His power work through us. Once people get a taste of serving, they often find themselves waiting with anticipation for God to open doors that they can jump through rather than waiting in fear for Him to push them through them.

5. **Serving allows us to experience God's presence in new ways.**

"Heal the sick, raise the dead, cleanse those who have leprosy, drive out demons. Freely you have received, freely give." (Matthew 10:5-8) When we bless others, we are blessed. When we encourage others, we find ourselves encouraged. When we see others healed and participate with prayer and the laying on of hands, we feel the miracle even more strongly.

Everyone has a different excuse not to serve, and we have heard (and some of us have said) them all:

I do not have time.
That is not my gift.
They already have so many people, I am not needed.
I do not know what I would do.

Remember this: Paul killed Christians. David was an adulterer. Moses was a murderer. None of the men above believed they were worthy of the calling God had placed on their lives. All of them tried to make excuses as to why they were not the right ones, and honestly, their reasons were right.

Not one of the "heroes of the faith" deserved the calling that God had placed on their lives. All of them were sinners. All of them were weak men. None were righteous.

God called them anyway and they answered.

God gave them His power, His might, His spirit, and because of Him, they changed the world. God does not want you to rely on your own strength. He wants to give you His.

The greatest commandments are to love God and love others. Jesus himself told us that the greatest love we can show for others is to be willing to lay down our lives for them. So, serve others. Why? Because it is how we can obey the greatest commandment God ever gave us, and how we can show love to others as Christ did.

DEEP DIVE QUESTIONS

- Have you ever volunteered to serve anywhere? (Does not have to be in a church) How did it make you feel?
- In what role do you feel more comfortable – the person doing the serving, or the person being served? Why do you think that is?
- Why do you think that people sometimes have problems getting "plugged in" to serve in a church?

NOTES

_____

_____

_____

_____

_____

_____

Congratulations on reaching the last sessions of *Walking Together – Steps to Discipleship*. You walked the journey from salvation to baptism and claimed the components of living an active Christian lifestyle. I hope that you have learned a lot and that you are putting into practice all that you have learned, because when we dive into the next four weeks, you may find yourself needing the endurance that you have been developing.

It is time to get messy. It is time to attack those subjects that send many Christian teachers running from their Bible in fear because they do not want to teach the hard stuff – the stuff that is difficult, scary, and sometimes hard to understand.

During the next 4 weeks, we will be traversing a very narrow tightrope with the following subjects:

1. **Spiritual Warfare**
2. **Gifts vs. Spiritual Fruit**
3. **Protecting my Witness (How what I say, think, and do matters in the Kingdom)**
4. **You have been re-made, now re-make others!**

When we claim our faith in Christ and begin to live an active lifestyle for Him, we will be challenged and attacked on every side. What we will learn during these next four weeks is that God has already placed within us everything we need to fight those battles and win. We will see the practical application of what we have been learning for the last eight weeks: We are now a part of an army, marching together as family to advance the Kingdom, and being a disciple of the Most High can sometimes be difficult.

The goal of any disciple of Jesus should be to re-create this process for someone else. We have been given a gift unlike any other and we have been charged by our Savior to go and make disciples of every nation. So, let us learn how we can prepare ourselves for just such a task!!!!!

*Be strong in the Lord and in His might, and put
on all of God's armor so that you will be able to stand
firm against all strategies of the devil. For we are not
fighting against flesh-and-blood enemies, but against
evil rulers and authorities of the unseen world,
against mighty powers in the dark world, and against
evil spirits in the heavenly places.*
Ephesians 6: 10-12

Ok, I am just going to say it. Demons are real. Satan is real. The powers of darkness are real. In addition, those forces are actively working against what God is doing in this world, and in the body of Christ. I am not going to lie; it is a very real war with casualties. The Devil hates you. He wants to steal, kill, and destroy. You, in your own strength do not have the ability to stand against him and his demons.

I am going to start with a very bold statement. You, as a spirit-filled believer, already have everything within you to defend yourself against the attacks of the devil. Paul begins the verses in Ephesians by telling us to be strong in the Lord. The Lord is within us. Allow yourself to be continually strengthened by the power already available to you through your faith in Jesus. He then tells you just how to do that, and it is the ultimate strategy in spiritual warfare.

Tongues? Nope

Deliverance? Nope

Is it through any other manifestation mentioned throughout the Bible? Nope

It is by putting on the FULL ARMOR OF GOD so that we may "stand firm against the strategies of the devil." The question is do we know how to recognize them and, if necessary, go to combat against the devil and his strategies? Well, since this is Warfare 101, I am going to start with five basic truths that the Bible teaches about Spiritual Warfare.

1. **There is an invisible world surrounding you that is just as real as the visible world.**

    There is a world that is as real as touching your skin, kissing your child, or watching a sunset. In the book of 2 Kings, it tells the story of Elisha and his servant being surrounded by a king and his army, and Elisha telling his servant not to worry because there were more with them than against them. The servant must have thought Elisha was crazy, but when Elisha prayed that the servant's eyes be opened, he saw that the hills around them were filled with horses and chariots of fire all around them. The point is that there are worlds surrounding us that we cannot see but are as real as what our senses can take in.

2. **We are involved in an invisible war that has been being waged for millennia and has eternal effects.**

    In 2 Corinthians 10 (NKJV), Paul writes, *"For although we walk in the flesh, we do not war according to the flesh. For the weapons of our warfare are not carnal but mighty in God for pulling down strongholds, casting down arguments and every high thing that exalts itself against the knowledge of God."* What Paul is saying is that while we may think that warfare is something out of the Exorcist movies, most of the battles will take place in our own hearts and minds.

3. **Our foe is formidable.**

    Satan in real. 1 Peter 5:8 (NASB1995) tells us that, *"our enemy, the devil, prowls the earth like a roaring lion, seeking whom he may devour."* Satan was a created angel of the highest order who was given the job as guardian of God's glory. HE let his pride motivate him to desire to be exalted over the throne of God. His pride caused him and one-third of the angels to be swept to earth. He and his angels have been working

against the Kingdom from the beginning and they try
to hit us in our deepest fears to cause us to lose sight
of our greatest weapon, Christ living in us. The devil
knows he must distract us, disconnect us, and discour-
age us from claiming our birthright as a child and ser-
vant of the Most-High.

4.   **Our foe is to be respected, but not feared.**

Did you hear that? Respect him, but do not fear him.
Be aware of his methods, but do not become preoc-
cupied by them. Paul says in 2 Corinthians 2:10-11
(TPT) that *"And if I have forgiven anything, I did so
for you before the face of Christ, so that we would not
be exploited by the adversary, Satan, for we know his
clever schemes."* He attacks governments, deceives
men, destroys life, persecutes the saints, prevents service, promotes division, and plants doubts. He pro-
vokes feelings of anger, pride, worry, self-reliance, dis-
couragement, worldliness, lying, immorality, and as
always, his battlefield is our minds and hearts. However, here is the silver lining - Satan's power is limited
and we have a greater power within us than he has.

5.   **As believers, we do not fight for victory – we fight
FROM victory.**

In Christ's power, we are INVINCIBLE. You are not
going into battle against Satan trying to win. You have
already won. 1 John 4:4 (ESV) – *"Greater is He who is
in you than he that is in the world."* 1 John 5:4-5 (NKJV)
— *"For whatever is born of God overcomes the world,
and this is the victory that did overcome the world, our
faith."* Finally, Revelation 12:11 — *"And they overcame
him (Satan) by the blood of the lamb and the word of
their testimony."*

Your greatest power. Your greatest weapon. The key
to spiritual warfare is that you are God's child. You are His
sons and daughters. Jesus faced the devil in the wilderness
and did not go all power and glory on him to defeat him,
he simply said, "It is written" and showed that the word

of God wins. Moreover, when Jesus says "It is written" or you say, "It is written," the authority of Scripture is over the demonic forces. They are UNDER YOUR FEET. There is nothing to be afraid of

So, to sum this all up... Satan and his demons are a defeated foe. Jesus destroyed the works of the devil and we are victors in Christ and have the power to resist Satan and his demonic attacks. We must gird ourselves with the armor of God through the scripture and by living an active, committed Christian lifestyle if we want to experience daily living in the victory THAT WE ALREADY POSSESS. Our ultimate weapon and our ultimate posture in Spiritual Warfare is to make sure that we have the strongest foundation possible, built on the ROCK. Knowing and claiming who you are in Christ is enough to equip you to overcome any attack of the enemy. So, fall in and get prepared for battle by realizing that you are already equipped beyond your wildest dreams.

DEEP DIVE QUESTIONS

- Do you find it difficult to believe that there are battles going on outside of what you can see?
- Do you feel equipped to go to war? Why or why not?
- What battles are you fighting right now? Have you used your best weapon yet? What scriptures have helped you in these moments?

NOTES

_____

_____

_____

_____

_____

_____

_____

_____

_____

_____

_____

_____

_____

_____

_____

_____

There are diversities of gifts, but the same Spirit."
For to one is give the word of wisdom through the
Spirit, to another the word of knowledge through the
same Spirit to another faith by the same Spirit, to
another gifts of healings by the same Spirit, to another
the working of miracles, to another prophecy, to
another discerning of spirits, to another different kinds
of tongues, to another the interpretation of tongues.
But one and the same Spirit works all these things,
distributing to each one individually as He wills.
1 Corinthians 12:4-11 (NKJV)

But the fruit of the Spirit is love, joy, peace,
patience, kindness, goodness, faithfulness gentleness,
self-control. Never set the law above these qualities,
for they are meant to be limitless.
Galatians 5:22-23 (TPT)

Never in the history of the church have the gifts of the Holy Spirit been pushed and studied more than today. We are taught to seek gifts and strive to manifest these gifts. What we lack as the body of Christ is an understanding of the fruits of this same Spirit. The problem with that is that they are connected intimately, and one cannot fully be utilized without the other.

The key to the verse in Corinthians is not the description of the gifts, but the knowledge that they are given at the will of the Holy Spirit. He may give one person the word of wisdom and to another the gift of healing. The key word here is that they are all gifts. You can strive for them and ask them, but nothing you do will bring them to you unless the Holy Spirit desires it. Gifts always confirm the Word of the Lord. In other words, whether you receive a word of wisdom, a word of knowledge, a prophecy, or speak in tongues, it is intended to prove what God is saying to you and doing through you.

The fruit of the Spirit is the demonstration of our "newness" in Christ as it is expressed to others through our actions. Galatians lists these fruits, and seeing these fruits played out in our very lives is the ultimate desire of the Father for His children. This may sound harsh, but it does not matter whether you speak in tongues or if you prophesy. Jesus is coming back to connect with those who possess His own nature; and that goes far beyond merely exercising spiritual gifts.

Consider what the Word of God says in Matthew 7:22-23 (NKJV) — *"Man will say to Me in that day, Lord, Lord, have we not prophesied in Your name, cast out demons in Your name, and done many wonders in Your name?" And then I will declare to them, I never knew you; depart from Me, you who practice lawlessness!"*

This tells us you can be actively serving yet refuse to deal with character issues – and this could disqualify you from doing God's work. We need to do regular "fruit-checks," because developing the "fruit of the Spirit" lays the proper foundation needed to operate in the things of God.

Too many believers have learned to speak "Christianese" way too well. We have become skilled at praising the Lord in church services, and then doing whatever we want to do afterwards. An old Pastor friend used to say, "You cannot behave like a saint on Sunday and a Saint Bernard the rest of the week." We have become so professional that we justify our lack of fruit. We make excuses for our behavior like, "That's just my personality... that's how I am."

There is a reason that 1 Corinthians 13 follows 1 Corinthians 12. Chapter 12 deals with and lists the gifts of the spirit, and then Paul lets us know in Chapter 13 that love is the ultimate gift of the spirit. If we practice any of the gifts of the spirit without the love of God expressed through our actions and without love as a result, then those gifts and manifestations are useless except to make us look "spiritual."

In Galatians 5:6 (TPT), the word tells us *"All that matters is living in the faith that works through love."* When we exercise our gifts, it should flow from a well of love for God's people. We should relate to each other from a spirit of love.

So, how can we develop the fruits of the Spirit in our lives?

1. **Go directly to the Source.**

   Developing the fruit of the spirit comes from a relationship with the Lord. Developing the fruit of the spirit becomes a natural process when we yield to the Lord. By spending time and developing a relationship with Him, appreciating how much He loves us, and understanding who He is and who He wants to be in us, we begin to yield to Jesus. That process allows us to develop a oneness with Him that results in us developing the fruit of the spirit.

2. **Remove any Barriers.**

   When we allow the Lord to work in our lives, areas of weakness will inevitably become known. The Lord will suggest areas that need His healing—offenses that must be forgiven, habits that need to be broken, and directions that we should follow. We may not even understand the reason for what the Lord tells us to do, but if we obey Him, the results will be life changing.

3. **Put Your Fruit on the Tree.**

   The reality is that fruit on a tree is not fruit until it is hanging on the branches. It is the same with spiritual fruit. We cannot claim to have fruit in our lives until we are willing to put it on display. We do not have the fruit of patience until we exhibit the fruit of patience. We do not have the fruit of faithfulness until we exhibit the fruit of faithfulness. Just as fruit on a tree starts small and grows, the fruit of the spirit must grow, too. When we develop our relationships with the Lord and remove blockages, we create a healthy spiritual environment that encourages growth.

4. **Realize that it is all about Jesus.**

Demonstrating the fruits in our lives should be the desire of every Christian because every Christian should want more of Jesus. As the book of Acts makes so clear: *"It is through Him that we live and function and have our identity; just as your own poets have said, 'Our lineage comes from Him'"* (Acts 17:28, TPT). That is why it is so important to allow Jesus to work in us. His presence in our lives becomes all-encompassing. When we need the fruit of the spirit, it is there for us because Jesus is in us.

The goal or both gifts and fruit is simple - Be more like Christ. We must return to the Bible so that it can work within us and reveal to us who we are in HIM so that we can see and fight against the shortcomings we may possess. You and I must learn our Bible so well that regardless of the circumstance, our "fruit" shines through.

Deep Dive Questions

- Why do you think that the modern church focuses so heavily on Spiritual Gifts?
- Do you think that up until now, you have chased after the giftings of God or the fruits? Why?
- Which of the steps of developing the Fruits of the Spirit do you have the most difficulty with? Why?

NOTES

_____

_____

_____

_____

_____

_____

_____

_____

_____

_____

_____

_____

_____

Week 11 –
Protecting my Witness

(How What I say, think and do matters to the Kingdom)

*"And they have conquered him by the blood of
the Lamb and by the word of their testimony, for they
loved not their lives even unto death."*
Revelation 12:11 (KJV)

One of the hardest things to digest when beginning a life trying to walk in purpose with God is realizing that whether we think we signed up for it or not, we now live in a fishbowl. People who hear of our newfound faith will be watching, either for confirmation of the change within us or to find evidence that we have not changed at all. We are walking a tightrope because we never know if the person standing in front of us or watching us walk by is someone that the Holy Spirit is placing in our path.

When asked what the greatest commandment is, Jesus responds that it is to Love the Lord, your God with all your heart, all of your soul, all of your mind, and all of your strength and the second is like it, we must love our neighbor as ourselves. Love God and love people. That sounds simple, but we also know that Jesus tells us that the greatest love we can give someone else is to lay down our lives for them. That sounds a little more complicated.

For those of you who are wondering, Jesus is not telling us to find ways to end our lives. However, he is asking it to give up our OLD LIVES AND HABITS. He is asking us to end all that used to keep us from Him. The Holy Spirit is a change agent. If he truly lives in our hearts, then we are a new creation. It just makes sense that if we are a new creation, we should behave as such.

The number one reason that is given by people who say they do not go to church is the hypocrisy that lies inside the walls. We all know what that means; people who live one way on Sunday and another way the rest of the week. The gossip, the backbiting, the division. If you have not experienced it, then consider yourself lucky.

The question is, what can we do to stop ourselves from being "that Christian"? How can we walk the tightrope? How can we ensure that we love people where they are? How can we be a true witness for Christ? The answer may be simpler and more difficult than you think. As a Christian, we must be "Christ-like."

Here are the easiest ways to protect your testimony in this modern, crazy world.

1. **Be careful with social media.**

   With the rise of social media, it can be easy to forget just how heavy the implications of the things we post, like, share or even just view have on our testimony. Social media has become more than just an accessory to our daily living. Even the extent to which you use it can speak loudly about what you really value most. You can destroy your entire witness with only a few keystrokes or an unwise post.

2. **Do not place value on material things.**

   God has a plan to give you a hope and a future, but He has this heart for everyone. The danger behind teachings that rely too heavily on prosperity is that they make people believe they are the center of the universe. But we are not. Jesus is the center of everything we do and that is the biblical emphasis on purpose that we must live out. Not what we gain, but what we lose for the sake of the Gospel.

3. **Do not let the world dictate what is right and wrong.**

   Just because we think something should be permissible, it does not make it so. Luke 17:2 (ESV) says, *"It would be better for him if a millstone were hung around his neck and he were cast into the sea than that he should cause one of these little ones to sin."* We MUST leave behind our old ways of relying on the world to tell us what is ok. Things like watching compromising movies and having certain relationships might not always be sinful. However, when we tread on the edge of a cliff, falling is much more likely and the people watching you could follow.

4. **Decide to only speak life.**

Proverbs 18:21 (ESV) tells us, *"Death and life are in the power of the tongue, and those who love it will eat its fruits."* There are only two things your tongue can speak, and if it is not speaking life, then it is definitely speaking death. With the words that you say, are you speaking life to others and adding to their value? When we fail to do so, we become a burden instead of being a blessing. Gossip, slander, lies, rudeness, sarcasm. All of these are weapons that the enemy will use to separate a lost soul from the Kingdom. Do not let yourself be a weapon of the enemy merely by opening your mouth. SPEAK LIFE. Love others with the very words you speak.

5. **Make sure your family has a strong foundation.**

While we may preach and champion the concept of faith in God, the way we conduct our family is one way that we live it out. When we fail to lead our families or to participate in a way that blesses the people closest to us, that speaks louder than any doctrine we can ever share. Our families and our children are our best witness. They are the greatest reflection of how we live our faith out in the day to day.

We must always strive to live righteously. Yes, the Bible tells us that other than Jesus, no one is truly righteous, but we must continually strive for that standard. We must care what others think about us. Not for popularity's sake, but for the sake of the Kingdom. We must be in the world, not of the world. We must walk, talk, think, speak, and live according to the standard set by Christ. We must do all we can to ensure that when people see us, they see Christ. Your words matter. How you treat others matters. Your actions are watched more than you know, both in the natural and the supernatural.

We must be constantly aware of this. Never forget that our ultimate purpose on earth is to glorify God and edify the body. If you ever wonder whether something you are doing or thinking is wrong, then ask yourself, "Is this glorifying God or edifying the body?" If the answer is no, then change. You already have the power of Christ within you. The Holy Spirit calls you His home, and He wants nothing more than to direct your heart and mind towards the very nature of who God is. So, let Him, and watch your witness grow beyond anything you thought possible.

Deep Dive Questions

- What are some things that the world tells us are ok, but you KNOW are wrong?
- What are three changes in your behaviors that you could make TODAY that you know would improve your witness to others?
- Can you think of three people (family, friends, co-workers) that you know need the change that you have experienced in their lives?

NOTES:

_____

_____

_____

_____

_____

_____

_____

_____

_____

_____

_____

_____

> *"Therefore, go into all the world and make disci-*
> *ples of all nations, baptizing them in the name of the*
> *Father and of the Son and of the Holy Spirit."*
> Matthew 28:19

I was told once by an old preacher friend of mine that people most often will remember the first thing you say, and the last thing you say. Last words are important – and the words in Matthew 28 were some of the last words that Jesus chose to say to His disciples before ascending to Heaven. Something tells me that they are pretty important for us as followers to remember.

The ultimate last step of any true journey to discipleship is to then begin helping others to become disciples themselves. The definition of a disciple is "a follower or student of a teacher, leader, or philosopher." To call ourselves disciples of Jesus means literally that we are to study His Word and ways and to follow His example. It is not just a word or a title. It is a choice and a lifestyle.

Here are some things we all need to understand about making disciples:

1. **Christ calls EVERYONE to make disciples.**

    Making disciples is not reserved for priests, ministers, reverends, pastors, or any of the other titles that people have given to those who shepherd congregations. The day Jesus ascended; it is reported by many that there were over five hundred people that witnessed it. Other sources say it was only the twelve disciples and Mary Magdalene. What we do know is that not all of those present were pastors or officially "titled" people. They were ordinary people who had answered His call, listened to His words, and followed His way.

That tells me that it is my job, too. I have heard and been taught His words and followed in His ways. He called to every follower who was, is, and ever will be to make disciples of ALL nations.

2. **There is not a magic formula or method to making a disciple.**

It is tempting for someone who is writing a study on taking steps towards Discipleship to claim that his is the ONLY WAY! But it isn't. It does not really matter if you have gone through your church's 12-week leadership and discipleship class with accountability partners and signed agreements, or if you simply developed an amazing discipling relationship with a co-worker or friend who led you to Christ and helped you find your way. Discipleship is intensely personal and involves a commitment to live life with the ONE who made us. How you get there is not the important part.

3. **Discipleship is a PROCESS**

If you are looking for a quick fix, discipleship is not for you. Every part of this process from renewing your mind to learning the disciplines of prayer and fasting takes TIME. It takes real commitment. I know that living in a fast-food, YouTube, do-it-yourself generation has made us all long for instant gratification. God desires a fire within you that is sustained and fueled over a LIFETIME of living and learning. Hebrews 12:1-2 says *"Therefore, since we are surrounded by such a great cloud of witnesses, let us throw off everything that hinders and the sin that so easily entangles. And let us run with perseverance the race marked out for us, fixing our eyes on Jesus, the pioneer and perfecter of faith. For the joy set before him he endured the cross, scorning its shame, and sat down at the right hand of the throne of God."* Jesus endured thing for us and asks that we be willing to ENDURE for Him.

4. **Never stop growing in your own Discipleship**

If discipleship is a process, then we should realize that it does not end until we reach our heavenly
reward! We all start with a goal to become closer to
Christ, then our goal is to become Christ-like. Well,
unless you have started walking on water you still
have a way to go! We are never supposed to stop reading, praying, learning, and serving. So, while you are
mentoring others and helping them to find the truths
of God, make sure you are taking the time you need to
continue your own process.

5. **Finally, remember that it is the Holy Spirit that is
doing the work.**

Let me say this as plainly as possible. YOU CANNOT
SAVE ANYONE! You did not live a perfect life, die on
the cross, or rise again on the third day. The work of
salvation was completed two thousand years ago on a
mountain in Jerusalem. You also were not sent by the
Father to be the comforter, counselor, or to reveal the
Spiritual Giftings of others. Those things were already
accomplished by Jesus and the Holy Spirit.

Here is what you **CAN** do!

You can help, listen, love, pray for, and serve as an
example to others of what it is like to cross from darkness
to light and from sin to salvation. You can serve as a witness to the power of the God that loves them, Jesus who
died for them, and the Spirit that now dwells within you
and can just as easily dwell within them if they keep following the Word and example of Christ.

DEEP DIVE QUESTIONS

- I know it may be early in your journey, but how comfortable on a scale of 1-10 are you in sharing your faith with others?
- Did you think once you reached salvation that you were done? Does it feel good to know that you still have more to do?
- I want you to write down the names of *at least* three people that you feel you could be a part of discipling to a closer relationship with Christ. Why did you choose who you did?

NOTES

_____

_____

_____

_____

_____

_____

_____

_____

Writing this study has been a challenging, cleansing, soul-searching experience for me. I will never forget kneeling at the chapel at West Virginia Wesleyan College and crying out to God and screaming like a mad man for God to come and change me from the inside out. Jesus met me there and did just that. I have embarked on a journey that has brought me here, 30+ years removed from that moment, and I still find myself with moments where I need guidance and insight from men and women of God that I trust. I am still on a continual process of a commitment to discipleship that I renew daily.

I remember clearly the saints that helped disciple me after my decision to accept Christ as my Savior and I hope in some way I can do the same for all of you through these pages.

I am an ordained Pastor, but I do not have a degree in theology, psychology, biblical studies, or any other subject that makes me someone you should necessarily listen to. I am just a guy that found Jesus and made a decision to follow and serve Him any way that He wanted.

The past churches that have heard me speak will tell you one thing about me – I never end anything I do without a chance for someone to come to salvation.

I have had the opportunity in my years of serving the Lord to meet a BUNCH of people of all ages, races, socioeconomic statuses, and stages of life. The one unwavering thing that each one of them had in common with me and with each other, and that they also have in common with you is– We all need Jesus.

If you have not met Him, meet Him now. Hear the gentle voice of the Holy Spirit as it calls to you. You are loved, called, chosen, and worthy of the love of a Heavenly Father that made you for a purpose. It does not take a church or an altar. Anywhere you open your heart and seek after God is the perfect place to receive Him. I hope you will do just that today.

I hope you have been encouraged and challenged by Walking Together – Steps towards Discipleship. I hope it has made a real difference in your walk. I hope that you realize that this journey was one that God prepared for you from the beginning, and He is with you on it every step of the way.

I hope you will feel comfortable enough to reach out via e-mail to me at Dcraig1010@yahoo.com. I would love to develop a relationship of prayer and mutual encouragement with anyone who ever reads these pages.

Grace and Peace,
Dennis Craig